Caligu

by C. Suetoniou

CAIUS CAESAR CALIGULA.

I. Germanicus, the father of Caius Caesar, and son of Drusus and the younger Antonia, was, after his adoption by Tiberius, his uncle, preferred to the quaestorship [377] five years before he had attained the legal age, and immediately upon the expiration of that office, to the consulship [378]. Having been sent to the army in Germany, he restored order among the legions, who, upon the news of Augustus's death, obstinately refused to acknowledge Tiberius as emperor [379], and offered to place him at the head of the state. In which affair it is difficult to say, whether his regard to filial duty, or the firmness of his resolution, was most conspicuous. Soon afterwards he defeated the enemy, and obtained the honours of a triumph. Being then made consul for the second time [380], before he could enter upon his office he was obliged to set out suddenly for the east, where, after he had conquered the king of Armenia, and reduced Cappadocia into the form of a province, he died at Antioch, of a lingering distemper, in the thirty-fourth year of his age [381], not without the suspicion of being poisoned. For besides the livid spots which appeared all over his body, and a foaming at the mouth; when his corpse was burnt, the heart was found entire among the bones; its nature being such, as it is supposed, that when tainted by poison, it is indestructible by fire. [382]

II. It was a prevailing opinion, that he was taken off by the contrivance of Tiberius, and through the means of Cneius Piso. This person, who was about the same time prefect of Syria, and made no secret of his position being such, that (252) he must either offend the father or the son, loaded Germanicus, even during his sickness, with the most unbounded and scurrilous abuse, both by word and deed; for which, upon his return to Rome, he narrowly escaped being torn to pieces by the people, and was condemned to death by the senate.

III. It is generally agreed, that Germanicus possessed all the noblest endowments of body and mind in a higher degree than had ever before fallen to the lot of any man; a handsome person, extraordinary courage, great proficiency in eloquence and other branches of learning, both Greek and Roman; besides a singular humanity, and a behaviour so engaging, as to captivate the affections of all about him. The slenderness of his legs did not correspond with the symmetry and beauty of his person in other respects; but this defect was at length corrected by his habit of riding after meals. In battle, he often engaged and slew an enemy in single combat. He pleaded causes, even after he had the honour of a triumph. Among other fruits of his studies, he left behind him some Greek comedies. Both at home and abroad he always conducted himself in a manner the most unassuming. On entering any free and confederate town, he never would be attended by his lictors. Whenever he heard, in his travels, of the tombs of illustrious men, he made offerings over them to the infernal deities. He gave a common grave, under a mound of earth, to the scattered relics of the legionaries slain under Varus, and was the first to put his hand to the work of collecting and bringing them to the place of burial. He was so extremely mild and gentle to his enemies, whoever they were, or on what account soever they bore him enmity, that, although Piso rescinded his decrees, and for a long time severely harassed his dependents, he never showed the smallest resentment, until he found himself attacked by magical charms and imprecations; and even then the only steps he took was to renounce all friendship with him, according to ancient custom, and to exhort his servants to avenge his death, if any thing untoward should befall him.

IV. He reaped the fruit of his noble qualities in abundance, being so much esteemed and beloved by his friends, that Augustus (to say nothing of his other relations) being a long time in doubt, whether he should not appoint him his successor, at last ordered Tiberius to adopt him. He was so extremely popular, that many authors tell us, the crowds of those who went to meet him upon his coming to any place, or to attend him at his departure, were so prodigious, that he was sometimes in danger of his life; and that upon his return from Germany, after he had quelled the mutiny in the army there, all the cohorts of the pretorian guards marched out to meet him, notwithstanding the order that only two should go; and that all the people of Rome, both men and women, of every age, sex, and rank, flocked as far as the twentieth milestone to attend his entrance.

V. At the time of his death, however, and afterwards, they displayed still greater and stronger proofs of their extraordinary attachment to him. The day on which he died, stones were thrown at the temples, the altars of the gods demolished, the household gods, in some cases, thrown into the streets, and new-born infants exposed. It is even said that barbarous nations, both those engaged in intestine wars, and those in hostilities against us, all agreed to a cessation of arms, as if they had been mourning for some very near and common friend; that some petty kings shaved their beards and their wives' heads, in token of their extreme sorrow; and that the king of kings [383] forbore his exercise of hunting and feasting with his nobles, which, amongst the Parthians, is equivalent to a cessation of all business in a time of public mourning with us.

VI. At Rome, upon the first news of his sickness, the city was thrown into great consternation and grief, waiting impatiently for farther intelligence; when suddenly, in the evening, a report, without any certain author, was spread, that he was recovered; upon which the people flocked with torches (254) and victims to the Capitol, and were in such haste to pay the vows they had made for his recovery, that they almost broke open the doors. Tiberius was roused from out of his sleep with the noise of the people congratulating one another, and singing about the streets,

Salva Roma, salva patria, salvus est Germanicus. Rome is safe, our country safe, for our Germanicus is safe.

But when certain intelligence of his death arrived, the mourning of the people could neither be assuaged by consolation, nor restrained by edicts, and it continued during the holidays in the month of December. The atrocities of the subsequent times contributed much to the glory of Germanicus, and the endearment of his memory; all people supposing, and with reason, that the fear and awe of him had laid a restraint upon the cruelty of Tiberius, which broke out soon afterwards.

VII. Germanicus married Agrippina, the daughter of Marcus Agrippa and Julia, by whom he had nine children, two of whom died in their infancy, and another a few years after; a sprightly boy, whose effigy, in the character of a Cupid, Livia set up in the temple of Venus in the Capitol. Augustus also placed another statue of him in his bed-chamber, and used to kiss it as often as he entered the apartment. The rest survived their father; three daughters, Agrippina, Drusilla, and Livilla, who were born in three successive years; and as many sons, Nero, Drusus, and Caius Caesar. Nero and Drusus, at the accusation of Tiberius, were declared public enemies.

VIII. Caius Caesar was born on the day before the calends [31st August] of September, at the time his father and Caius Fonteius Capito were consuls [384]. But where he was born, is rendered uncertain from the number of places which are said to have given him birth. Cneius Lentulus Gaetulicus [385] says that he was born at Tibur; Pliny the younger, in the country of the Treviri, at a village called Ambiatinus, above Confluentes [386]; and he alleges, as a proof of it, that altars are there shown with this inscription: "For Agrippina's child-birth." Some verses which were published in his reign, intimate that he was born in the winter quarters of the legions,

In castris natus, patriis nutritius in armis, Jam designati principis omen erat.

Born in the camp, and train'd in every toil Which taught his sire the haughtiest foes to foil; Destin'd he seem'd by fate to raise his name, And rule the empire with Augustan fame.

I find in the public registers that he was born at Antium. Pliny charges Gaetulicus as guilty of an arrant forgery, merely to soothe the vanity of a conceited young prince, by giving him the lustre of being born in a city sacred to Hercules; and says that he advanced this false assertion with the more assurance, because, the year before the birth of Caius, Germanicus had a son of the same name born at Tibur; concerning whose amiable childhood and premature death I have already spoken [387]. Dates clearly prove that Pliny is mistaken; for the writers of Augustus's history all agree, that Germanicus, at the expiration of his consulship, was sent into Gaul, after the birth of Caius. Nor will the inscription upon the altar serve to establish Pliny's opinion;

because Agrippina was delivered of two daughters in that country, and any child-birth, without regard to sex, is called puerperium, as the ancients were used to call girls puerae, and boys puelli. There is also extant a letter written by Augustus, a few months before his death, to his granddaughter Agrippina, about the same Caius (for there was then no other child of hers living under that name). He writes as follows: "I gave orders yesterday for Talarius and Asellius to set out on their journey towards you, if the gods permit, with your child Caius, upon the fifteenth of the calends of June [18th May]. I also send with him a physician of mine, and I wrote to Germanicus that he may retain him if he pleases. Farewell, my dear Agrippina, and take what care you can to (256) come safe and well to your Germanicus." I imagine it is sufficiently evident that Caius could not be born at a place to which he was carried from The City when almost two years old. The same considerations must likewise invalidate the evidence of the verses, and the rather, because the author is unknown. The only authority, therefore, upon which we can depend in this matter, is that of the acts, and the public register; especially as he always preferred Antium to every other place of retirement, and entertained for it all that fondness which is commonly attached to one's native soil. It is said, too, that, upon his growing weary of the city, he designed to have transferred thither the seat of empire.

IX. It was to the jokes of the soldiers in the camp that he owed the name of Caligula [388], he having been brought up among them in the dress of a common soldier. How much his education amongst them recommended him to their favour and affection, was sufficiently apparent in the mutiny upon the death of Augustus, when the mere sight of him appeased their fury, though it had risen to a great height. For they persisted in it, until they observed that he was sent away to a neighbouring city [389], to secure him against all danger. Then, at last, they began to relent, and, stopping the chariot in which he was conveyed, earnestly deprecated the odium to which such a proceeding would expose them.

X. He likewise attended his father in his expedition to Syria. After his return, he lived first with his mother, and, when she was banished, with his great-grandmother, Livia Augusta, in praise of whom, after only a boy, he pronounced a funeral oration in the e, though then transferred to the family of his grandmother, Antonia, and he was then twentieth year of his age, being called by Tiberius to Capri, ards, in the same day assumed the manly habit, and shaved his bear ne and the receiving any of the honours which had been paid to his brothers without (257) occasion. While he remained in that island, many insidiou similar were practised, to extort from him complaints against Tiberius, but his circumspection he avoided falling into the snare [390]. He affected to tak no more notice of the ill-treatment of his relations, than if nothing had befalle. them. With regard to his own sufferings, he seemed utterly insensible of them, and behaved with such obsequiousness to his grandfather [391] and all about him, that it was justly said of him, "There never was a better servant, nor a worse master."

XI. But he could not even then conceal his natural disposition to cruelty and lewdness. He delighted in witnessing the infliction of punishments, and frequented taverns and bawdy-houses in the night-time, disguised in a periwig and a long coat; and was passionately addicted to the theatrical arts of singing and dancing. All these levities Tiberius readily connived at, in hopes that they might perhaps correct the roughness of his temper, which the sagacious old man so well understood, that he often said, "That Caius was destined to be the ruin of himself and all mankind; and that he was rearing a hydra [392] for the people of Rome, and a Phaeton for all the world." [393]

XII. Not long afterwards, he married Junia Claudilla, the daughter of Marcus Silanus, a man of the highest rank. Being then chosen augur in the room of his brother Drusus, before he could be inaugurated he was advanced to the pontificate, with no small commendation of his dutiful behaviour, and great capacity. The situation of the court likewise was at this time favourable to his fortunes, as it was now left destitute of support, Sejanus being suspected, and soon afterwards taken off; and he was by degrees flattered with the hope of succeeding Tiberius in the empire. In order more effectually to secure this object, upon Junia's dying in child-bed, he engaged in a criminal commerce

, the wife (258) of Macro, at that time prefect of the *with Enni* promising to marry her if he became emperor, to which he *pretorian* not only by an oath, but by a written obligation under his hand. *bound h..r* means insinuated himself into Macro's favour, some are of *Having* he attempted to poison Tiberius, and ordered his ring to be taken *opinio* before the breath was out of his body; and that, because he seemed *from* t fast, he caused a pillow to be thrown upon him [394], squeezing him *to h* throat, at the same time, with his own hand. One of his freedmen crying *by* at this horrid barbarity, he was immediately crucified. These circumstances are far from being improbable, as some authors relate that, afterwards, though he did not acknowledge his having a hand in the death of Tiberius, yet he frankly declared that he had formerly entertained such a design; and as a proof of his affection for his relations, he would frequently boast, "That, to revenge the death of his mother and brothers, he had entered the chamber of Tiberius, when he was asleep, with a poniard, but being seized with a fit of compassion, threw it away, and retired; and that Tiberius, though aware of his intention, durst not make any inquiries, or attempt revenge."

XIII. Having thus secured the imperial power, he fulfilled by his elevation the wish of the Roman people, I may venture to say, of all mankind; for he had long been the object of expectation and desire to the greater part of the provincials and soldiers, who had known him when a child; and to the whole people of Rome, from their affection for the memory of Germanicus, his father, and compassion for the family almost entirely destroyed. Upon his moving from Misenum, therefore, although he was in mourning, and following the corpse of Tiberius, he had to walk amidst altars, victims, and lighted torches, with prodigious crowds of people everywhere attending him, in transports of joy, and calling him, besides other auspicious names, by those of "their star," "their chick," "their pretty puppet," and "bantling."

XIV. Immediately on his entering the city, by the joint acclamations of the senate, and people, who broke into the senate-house, Tiberius's will was set aside, it having left his (259) other grandson [395], then a minor, coheir with him, the whole government and administration of affairs was placed in his hands; so much to the joy and satisfaction of the public, that, in less than three months after, above a hundred and sixty thousand victims are said to have been offered in sacrifice. Upon his going, a few days afterwards, to the nearest islands on the coast of Campania [396], vows were made for his safe return; every person emulously testifying their care and concern for his safety. And when he fell ill, the people hung about the Palatium all night long; some vowed, in public handbills, to risk their lives in the combats of the amphitheatre, and others to lay them down, for his recovery. To this extraordinary love entertained for him by his countrymen, was added an uncommon regard by foreign nations. Even Artabanus, king of the Parthians, who had always manifested hatred and contempt for Tiberius, solicited his friendship; came to hold a conference with his consular lieutenant, and passing the Euphrates, paid the highest honours to the eagles, the Roman standards, and the images of the Caesars. [397]

XV. Caligula himself inflamed this devotion, by practising all the arts of popularity. After he had delivered, with floods of tears, a speech in praise of Tiberius, and buried him with the utmost pomp, he immediately hastened over to Pandataria and the Pontian islands [398], to bring thence the ashes of his mother and brother; and, to testify the great regard he had for their memory, he performed the voyage in a very tempestuous season. He approached their remains with profound veneration, and deposited them in the urns with his own hands. Having brought them in grand solemnity to Ostia [399], with an ensign flying in the stern of the galley, and thence up the Tiber to Rome, they were borne by persons of the first distinction in the equestrian order, on two biers, into the mausoleum [400], (260) at noon-day. He appointed yearly offerings to be solemnly and publicly celebrated to their memory, besides Circensian games to that of his mother, and a chariot with her image to be included in the procession [401]. The month of September he called Germanicus, in honour of his father. By a single decree of the senate, he heaped upon his grandmother, Antonia, all the honours which had been ever conferred on the empress Livia. His uncle, Claudius, who till then continued in the equestrian order, he took for his colleague in the consulship. He adopted his brother, Tiberius [402], on the day he took upon him the manly habit, and conferred upon him the title of "Prince of the Youths." As for his sisters, he ordered these words to be added to the oaths of allegiance to himself: "Nor will I hold myself or my own children more dear than I do Caius and his sisters:" [403] and commanded all resolutions proposed by the consuls in the senate to be prefaced thus: "May what we are going to do, prove fortunate and happy to Caius Caesar and his sisters." With the like popularity he restored all those who had been condemned and banished, and granted an act of indemnity against all impeachments and past offences. To relieve the informers and witnesses against his mother and brothers from all apprehension, he brought the records of their trials into the forum, and there burnt them, calling loudly on the gods to witness that he had not read or handled them. A memorial which was offered him relative to his own security, he would not receive, declaring, "that he had done nothing to make any one his enemy:" and said, at the same time, "he had no ears for informers."

XVI. The Spintriae, those panderers to unnatural lusts [404], he banished from the city, being prevailed upon not to throw them (261) into the sea, as he had intended. The writings of Titus Labienus, Cordus Cremutius, and Cassius Severus, which had been suppressed by an act of the senate, he permitted to be drawn from obscurity, and universally read; observing, "that it would be for his own advantage to have the transactions of former times delivered to posterity." He published accounts of the proceedings of the government--a practice which had been introduced by Augustus, but discontinued by Tiberius [405]. He granted the magistrates a full and free jurisdiction, without any appeal to himself. He made a very strict and exact review of the Roman knights, but conducted it with moderation; publicly depriving of his horse every knight who lay under the stigma of any thing base and dishonourable; but passing over the names of those knights who were only guilty of venial faults, in calling over the list of the order. To lighten the labours of the judges, he added a fifth class to the former four. He attempted likewise to restore to the people their ancient right of voting in the choice of magistrates [406]. He paid very honourably, and without any dispute, the legacies left by Tiberius in his will, though it had been set aside; as likewise those left by the will of Livia Augusta, which Tiberius had annulled. He remitted the hundredth penny, due to the government in all auctions throughout Italy. He made up to many their losses sustained by fire; and when he restored their kingdoms to any princes, he likewise allowed them all the arrears of the taxes and revenues which had accrued in the interval; as in the case of Antiochus of Comagene, where the confiscation would have amounted to a hundred millions of sesterces. To prove to the world that he was ready to encourage good examples of every kind, he gave to a freed-woman eighty thousand sesterces, for not discovering a crime committed by her patron, though she had been put to exquisite torture for that purpose. For all these acts of beneficence, amongst other honours, a golden shield was decreed to him, which the colleges of priests were to carry annually, upon a fixed day, into the Capitol, with the senate attending, and the youth of the nobility, of both sexes, celebrating the praise of his virtues in (262) songs. It was likewise ordained, that the day on which he succeeded to the empire should be called Palilia, in token of the city's being at that time, as it were, new founded. [407]

XVII. He held the consulship four times; the first [408], from the calends [the first] of July for two months: the second [409], from the calends of January for thirty days; the third [410], until the ides [the 13th] of January; and the fourth [411], until the seventh of the same ides [7th January]. Of these, the two last he held successively. The third he assumed by his sole authority at Lyons; not, as some are of opinion, from arrogance or neglect of rules; but because, at that distance, it was impossible for him to know that his colleague had died a little before the beginning of the new year. He twice distributed to the people a bounty of three hundred sesterces a man, and as often gave a splendid feast to the senate and the equestrian order, with their wives and children. In the latter, he presented to the men forensic garments, and to the women and children purple scarfs. To make a perpetual addition to the public joy for ever, he added to the Saturnalia [412] one day, which he called Juvenalis [the juvenile feast].

XVIII. He exhibited some combats of gladiators, either in the amphitheatre of Taurus [413], or in the Septa, with which he intermingled troops of the best pugilists from Campania and Africa. He did not always preside in person upon those occasions, but sometimes gave a commission to magistrates or friends to supply his place. He frequently entertained the people with stage-plays (263) of various kinds, and in several parts of the city, and sometimes by night, when he caused the whole city to be lighted. He likewise gave various things to be scrambled for among the people, and distributed to every man a basket of bread with other victuals. Upon this occasion, he sent his own share to a Roman knight, who was seated opposite to him, and was enjoying himself by eating heartily. To a senator, who was doing the same, he sent an appointment of praetor-extraordinary. He likewise exhibited a great number of Circensian games from morning until night; intermixed with the hunting of wild beasts from Africa, or the Trojan exhibition. Some of these games were celebrated with peculiar circumstances; the Circus being overspread with vermilion and chrysolite; and none drove in the chariot races who were not of the senatorian order. For some of these he suddenly gave the signal, when, upon his viewing from the Gelotiana [414] the preparations in the Circus, he was asked to do so by a few persons in the neighbouring galleries.

XIX. He invented besides a new kind of spectacle, such as had never been heard of before. For he made a bridge, of about three miles and a half in length, from Baiae to the mole of Puteoli [415], collecting trading vessels from all quarters, mooring them in two rows by their anchors, and spreading earth upon them to form a viaduct, after the fashion of the Appian Way [416]. This bridge he crossed and recrossed for two days together; the first day mounted on a horse richly caparisoned, wearing on his head a crown of oak leaves, armed with a battle-axe, a Spanish buckler and a sword, and in a cloak made of cloth of gold; the day following, in the habit of a charioteer, standing in a chariot, drawn by two high-bred horses, having with him a young boy, Darius by name, one of the Parthian hostages, with a cohort of the pretorian guards attending him, and a (264) party of his friends in cars of Gaulish make [417]. Most people, I know, are of opinion, that this bridge was designed by Caius, in imitation of Xerxes, who, to the astonishment of the world, laid a bridge over the Hellespont, which is somewhat narrower than the distance betwixt Baiae and Puteoli. Others, however, thought that he did it to strike terror in Germany and Britain, which he was upon the point of invading, by the fame of some prodigious work. But for myself, when I was a boy, I heard my grandfather say [418], that the reason assigned by some courtiers who were in habits of the greatest intimacy with him, was this; when Tiberius was in some anxiety about the nomination of a successor, and rather inclined to pitch upon his grandson, Thrasyllus the astrologer had assured him, "That Caius would no more be emperor, than he would ride on horseback across the gulf of Baiae."

XX. He likewise exhibited public diversions in Sicily, Grecian games at Syracuse, and Attic plays at Lyons in Gaul besides a contest for pre- eminence in the Grecian and Roman eloquence; in which we are told that such as were baffled bestowed rewards upon the best performers, and were obliged to compose speeches in their praise: but that those who performed the worst, were forced to blot out what they had written with a sponge or their tongue, unless they preferred to be beaten with a rod, or plunged over head and ears into the nearest river.

XXI. He completed the works which were left unfinished by Tiberius, namely, the temple of Augustus, and the theatre (265) of Pompey [419]. He began, likewise, the aqueduct from the neighbourhood of Tibur [420], and an amphitheatre near the Septa [421]; of which works, one was completed by his successor Claudius, and the other remained as he left it. The walls of Syracuse, which had fallen to decay by length of time, he repaired, as he likewise did the temples of the gods. He formed plans for rebuilding the palace of Polycrates at Samos, finishing the temple of the Didymaean Apollo at Miletus, and building a town on a ridge of the Alps; but, above all, for cutting through the isthmus in Achaia [422]; and even sent a centurion of the first rank to measure out the work.

XXII. Thus far we have spoken of him as a prince. What remains to be said of him, bespeaks him rather a monster than a man. He assumed a variety of titles, such as "Dutiful," "The (266) Pious," "The Child of the Camp, the Father of the Armies," and "The Greatest and Best Caesar." Upon hearing some kings, who came to the city to pay him court, conversing together at supper, about their illustrious descent, he exclaimed,

Eis koiranos eto, eis basileus. Let there be but one prince, one king.

He was strongly inclined to assume the diadem, and change the form of government, from imperial to regal; but being told that he far exceeded the grandeur of kings and princes, he began to arrogate to himself a divine majesty. He ordered all the images of the gods, which were famous either for their beauty, or the veneration paid them, among which was that of Jupiter Olympius, to be brought from Greece, that he might take the heads off, and put on his own. Having continued part of the Palatium as far as the Forum, and the temple of Castor and Pollux being converted into a kind of vestibule to his house, he often stationed himself between the twin brothers, and so presented himself to be worshipped by all votaries; some of whom saluted him by the name of Jupiter Latialis. He also instituted a temple and priests, with choicest victims, in honour of his own divinity. In his temple stood a statue of gold, the exact image of himself, which was daily dressed in garments corresponding with those he wore himself. The most opulent persons in the city offered themselves as candidates for the honour of being his priests, and purchased it successively at an immense price. The victims were flamingos, peacocks, bustards, guinea-fowls, turkey and pheasant hens, each sacrificed on their respective days. On nights when the moon was full, he was in the constant habit of inviting her to his embraces and his bed. In the day- time he talked in private to Jupiter Capitolinus; one while whispering to him, and another turning his ear to him: sometimes he spoke aloud, and in railing language. For he was overheard to threaten the god thus:

Hae em' anaeir', hae ego se; [423] Raise thou me up, or I'll--

(267) until being at last prevailed upon by the entreaties of the god, as he said, to take up his abode with him, he built a bridge over the temple of the Deified Augustus, by which he joined the Palatium to the Capitol. Afterwards, that he might be still nearer, he laid the foundations of a new palace in the very court of the Capitol.

XXIII. He was unwilling to be thought or called the grandson of Agrippa, because of the obscurity of his birth; and he was offended if any one, either in prose or verse, ranked him amongst the Caesars. He said that his mother was the fruit of an incestuous commerce, maintained by Augustus with his daughter Julia. And not content with this vile reflection upon the memory of Augustus, he forbad his victories at Actium, and on the coast of Sicily, to be celebrated, as usual; affirming that they had been most pernicious and fatal to the Roman people. He called his grandmother Livia Augusta "Ulysses in a woman's dress," and had the indecency to reflect upon her in a letter to the senate, as of mean birth, and descended, by the mother's side, from a grandfather who was only one of the municipal magistrates of Fondi; whereas it is certain, from the public records, that Aufidius Lurco held high offices at Rome. His grandmother Antonia desiring a private conference with him, he refused to grant it, unless Macro, the prefect of the pretorian guards, were present. Indignities of this kind, and ill usage, were the cause of her death; but some think he also gave her poison. Nor did he pay the smallest respect to her memory after her death, but witnessed the burning from his private apartment. His brother Tiberius, who had no expectation of any violence, was suddenly dispatched by a military tribune sent by his order for that purpose. He forced Silanus, his father-in-law, to kill himself, by cutting his throat with a razor. The pretext he alleged for these murders was, that the latter had not followed him upon his putting to sea in stormy weather, but stayed behind with the view of seizing the city, if he should perish. The other, he said, smelt of an antidote, which he had taken to prevent his being poisoned by him; whereas Silanus was only afraid of being sea-sick, and the disagreeableness of a voyage; and Tiberius had merely taken a medicine for an habitual cough, (268) which was continually growing worse. As for his successor Claudius, he only saved him for a laughing- stock.

XXIV. He lived in the habit of incest with all his sisters; and at table, when much company was present, he placed each of them in turns below him, whilst his wife reclined above him. It is believed, that he deflowered one of them, Drusilla, before he had assumed the robe of manhood; and was even caught in her embraces by his grandmother Antonia, with whom they were educated together. When she was afterwards married to Cassius Longinus, a man of consular rank, he took her from him, and kept her constantly as if she were his lawful wife. In a fit of sickness, he by his will appointed her heiress both of his estate and the empire. After her death, he ordered a public mourning for her; during which it was capital for any person to laugh, use the bath, or sup with his parents, wife, or children. Being inconsolable under his affliction, he went hastily, and in the night-time, from the City; going through Campania to Syracuse, and then suddenly returned without shaving his beard, or trimming his hair. Nor did he ever afterwards, in matters of the greatest importance, not even in the assemblies of the people or before the soldiers, swear any otherwise, than "By the divinity of Drusilla." The rest of his sisters he did not treat with so much fondness or regard; but frequently prostituted them to his catamites. He therefore the more readily condemned them in the case of Aemilius Lepidus, as guilty of adultery, and privy to that conspiracy against him. Nor did he only divulge their own hand-writing relative to the affair, which he procured by base and lewd means, but likewise consecrated to Mars the Avenger three swords which had been prepared to stab him, with an inscription, setting forth the occasion of their consecration.

XXV. Whether in the marriage of his wives, in repudiating them, or retaining them, he acted with greater infamy, it is difficult to say. Being at the wedding of Caius Piso with Livia Orestilla, he ordered the bride to be carried to his own house, but within a few days divorced her, and two years after banished her; because it was thought, that upon her divorce she returned to the embraces of her former husband. (269) Some say, that being invited to the wedding-supper, he sent a messenger to Piso, who sat opposite to him, in these words: "Do not be too fond with my wife," and that he immediately carried her off. Next day he published a proclamation, importing, "That he had got a wife as Romulus and Augustus had done." [424] Lollia Paulina, who was married to a man of consular rank in command of an army, he suddenly called from the province where she was with her husband, upon mention being made that her grandmother was formerly very beautiful, and married her; but he soon afterwards parted with her, interdicting her from having ever afterwards any commerce with man. He loved with a most passionate and constant affection Caesonia, who was neither handsome nor young; and was besides the mother of three daughters by another man; but a wanton of unbounded lasciviousness. Her he would frequently exhibit to the soldiers, dressed in a military cloak, with shield and helmet, and riding by his side. To his friends he even showed her naked. After she had a child, he honoured her with the title of wife; in one and the same day, declaring himself her husband, and father of the child of which she was delivered. He named it Julia Drusilla, and carrying it round the temples of all the goddesses, laid it on the lap of Minerva; to whom he recommended the care of bringing up and instructing her. He considered her as his own child for no better reason than her savage temper, which was such even in her infancy, that she would attack with her nails the face and eyes of the children at play with her.

XXVI. It would be of little importance, as well as disgusting, to add to all this an account of the manner in which he treated his relations and friends; as Ptolemy, king Juba's son, his cousin (for he was the grandson of Mark Antony by his daughter Selene) [425], and especially Macro himself, and Ennia likewise [426], by whose assistance he had obtained the empire; all of whom, for their alliance and eminent services, he rewarded with violent deaths. Nor was he more mild or respectful in his behaviour towards the senate. Some who had borne the (270) highest offices in the government, he suffered to run by his litter in their togas for several miles together, and to attend him at supper, sometimes at the head of his couch, sometimes at his feet, with napkins. Others of them, after he had privately put them to death, he nevertheless continued to send for, as if they were still alive, and after a few days pretended that they had laid violent hands upon themselves. The consuls having forgotten to give public notice of his birth-day, he displaced them; and the republic was three days without any one in that high office. A quaestor who was said to be concerned in a conspiracy against him, he scourged severely, having first stripped off his clothes, and spread them under the feet of the soldiers employed in the work, that they might stand the more firm. The other orders likewise he treated with the same insolence and violence. Being disturbed by the noise of people taking their places at midnight in the circus, as they were to have free admission, he drove them all away with clubs. In this tumult, above twenty Roman knights were squeezed to death, with as many matrons, with a great crowd besides. When stage-plays were acted, to occasion disputes between the people and the knights, he distributed the money-tickets sooner than usual, that the seats assigned to the knights might be all occupied by the mob. In the spectacles of gladiators, sometimes, when the sun was violently hot, he would order the curtains, which covered the amphitheatre, to be drawn aside [427], and forbad any person to be let out; withdrawing at the same time the usual apparatus for the entertainment, and presenting wild beasts almost pined to death, the most sorry gladiators, decrepit with age, and fit only to work the machinery, and decent house-keepers, who were remarkable for some bodily infirmity. Sometimes shutting up the public granaries, he would oblige the people to starve for a while.

XXVII. He evinced the savage barbarity of his temper chiefly by the following indications. When flesh was only to be had at a high price for feeding his wild beasts reserved for the spectacles, he ordered that criminals should be given them (271) to be devoured; and upon inspecting them in a row, while he stood in the middle of the portico, without troubling himself to examine their cases he ordered them to be dragged away, from "bald-pate to bald-pate." [428] Of one person who had made a vow for his recovery to combat with a gladiator, he exacted its performance; nor would he allow him to desist until he came off conqueror, and after many entreaties. Another, who had vowed to give his life for the same cause, having shrunk from the sacrifice, he delivered, adorned as a victim, with garlands and fillets, to boys, who were to drive him through the streets, calling on him to fulfil his vow, until he was thrown headlong from the ramparts. After disfiguring many persons of honourable rank, by branding them in the face with hot irons, he condemned them to the mines, to work in repairing the high-ways, or to fight with wild beasts; or tying them by the neck and heels, in the manner of beasts carried to slaughter, would shut them up in cages, or saw them asunder. Nor were these severities merely inflicted for crimes of great enormity, but for making remarks on his public games, or for not having sworn by the Genius of the emperor. He compelled parents to be present at the execution of their sons; and to one who excused himself on account of indisposition, he sent his own litter. Another he invited to his table immediately after he had witnessed the spectacle, and coolly challenged him to jest and be merry. He ordered the overseer of the spectacles and wild beasts to be scourged in fetters, during several days successively, in his own presence, and did not put him to death until he was disgusted with the stench of his putrefied brain. He burned alive, in the centre of the arena of the amphitheatre, the writer of a farce, for some witty verse, which had a double meaning. A Roman knight, who had been exposed to the wild beasts, crying out that he was innocent, he called him back, and having had his tongue cut out, remanded him to the arena.

XXVIII. Asking a certain person, whom he recalled after a long exile, how he used to spend his time, he replied, with flattery, "I was always praying the gods for what has happened, that Tiberius might die, and you be emperor." Concluding, therefore, that those he had himself banished also (272) prayed for his death, he sent orders round the islands [429] to have them all put to death. Being very desirous to have a senator torn to pieces, he employed some persons to call him a public enemy, fall upon him as he entered the senate-house, stab him with their styles, and deliver him to the rest to tear asunder. Nor was he satisfied, until he saw the limbs and bowels of the man, after they had been dragged through the streets, piled up in a heap before him.

XXIX. He aggravated his barbarous actions by language equally outrageous. "There is nothing in my nature," said he, "that I commend or approve so much, as my adiatrepsia (inflexible rigour)." Upon his grandmother Antonia's giving him some advice, as if it was a small matter to pay no regard to it, he said to her, "Remember that all things are lawful for me." When about to murder his brother, whom he suspected of taking antidotes against poison, he said, "See then an antidote against Caesar!" And when he banished his sisters, he told them in a menacing tone, that he had not only islands at command, but likewise swords. One of pretorian rank having sent several times from Anticyra [430], whither he had gone for his health, to have his leave of absence prolonged, he ordered him to be put to death; adding these words "Bleeding is necessary for one that has taken hellebore so long, and found no benefit." It was his custom every tenth day to sign the lists of prisoners appointed for execution; and this he called "clearing his accounts." And having condemned several Gauls and Greeks at one time, he exclaimed in triumph, "I have conquered Gallograecia." [431]

XXX. He generally prolonged the sufferings of his victims by causing them to be inflicted by slight and frequently repeated strokes; this being his well-known and constant order: (273) "Strike so that he may feel himself die." Having punished one person for another, by mistaking his name, he said, "he deserved it quite as much." He had frequently in his mouth these words of the tragedian,

Oderint dum metuant. [432] I scorn their hatred, if they do but fear me.

He would often inveigh against all the senators without exception, as clients of Sejanus, and informers against his mother and brothers, producing the memorials which he had pretended to burn, and excusing the cruelty of Tiberius as necessary, since it was impossible to question the veracity of such a number of accusers [433]. He continually reproached the whole equestrian order, as devoting themselves to nothing but acting on the stage, and fighting as gladiators. Being incensed at the people's applauding a party at the Circensian games in opposition to him, he exclaimed, "I wish the Roman people had but one neck." [434] When Tetrinius, the highwayman, was denounced, he said his persecutors too were all Tetrinius's. Five Retiarii [435], in tunics, fighting in a company, yielded without a struggle to the same number of opponents; and being ordered to be slain, one of them taking up his lance again, killed all the conquerors. This he lamented in a proclamation as a most cruel butchery, and cursed all those who had borne the sight of it.

XXXI. He used also to complain aloud of the state of the times, because it was not rendered remarkable by any public (274) calamities; for, while the reign of Augustus had been made memorable to posterity by the disaster of Varus [436], and that of Tiberius by the fall of the theatre at Fidenae [437], his was likely to pass into oblivion, from an uninterrupted series of prosperity. And, at times, he wished for some terrible slaughter of his troops, a famine, a pestilence, conflagrations, or an earthquake.

XXXII. Even in the midst of his diversions, while gaming or feasting, this savage ferocity, both in his language and actions, never forsook him. Persons were often put to the torture in his presence, whilst he was dining or carousing. A soldier, who was an adept in the art of beheading, used at such times to take off the heads of prisoners, who were brought in for that purpose. At Puteoli, at the dedication of the bridge which he planned, as already mentioned [438], he invited a number of people to come to him from the shore, and then suddenly, threw them headlong into the sea; thrusting down with poles and oars those who, to save themselves, had got hold of the rudders of the ships. At Rome, in a public feast, a slave having stolen some thin plates of silver with which the couches were inlaid, he delivered him immediately to an executioner, with orders to cut off his hands, and lead him round the guests, with them hanging from his neck before his breast, and a label, signifying the cause of his punishment. A gladiator who was practising with him, and voluntarily threw himself at his feet, he stabbed with a poniard, and then ran about with a palm branch in his hand, after the manner of those who are victorious in the games. When a victim was to be offered upon an altar, he, clad in the habit of the Popae [439], and holding the axe aloft for a while, at last, instead of the animal, slaughtered an officer who attended to cut up the sacrifice. And at a sumptuous entertainment, he fell suddenly into a violent fit of laughter, and upon the consuls, who reclined next to him, respectfully asking him the occasion, "Nothing," replied he, "but that, upon a single nod of mine, you might both have your throats cut."

(275) XXXIII. Among many other jests, this was one: As he stood by the statue of Jupiter, he asked Apelles, the tragedian, which of them he thought was biggest? Upon his demurring about it, he lashed him most severely, now and then commending his voice, whilst he entreated for mercy, as being well modulated even when he was venting his grief. As often as he kissed the neck of his wife or mistress, he would say, "So beautiful a throat must be cut whenever I please;" and now and then he would threaten to put his dear Caesonia to the torture, that he might discover why he loved her so passionately.

XXXIV. In his behaviour towards men of almost all ages, he discovered a degree of jealousy and malignity equal to that of his cruelty and pride. He so demolished and dispersed the statues of several illustrious persons, which had been removed by Augustus, for want of room, from the court of the Capitol into the Campus Martius, that it was impossible to set them up again with their inscriptions entire. And, for the future, he forbad any statue whatever to be erected without his knowledge and leave. He had thoughts too of suppressing Homer's poems: "For why," said he, "may not I do what Plato has done before me, who excluded him from his commonwealth?" [440] He was likewise very near banishing the writings and the busts of Virgil and Livy from all libraries; censuring one of them as "a man of no genius and very little learning;" and the other as "a verbose and careless historian." He often talked of the lawyers as if he intended to abolish their profession. "By Hercules!" he would say, "I shall put it out of their power to answer any questions in law, otherwise than by referring to me!"

XXXV. He took from the noblest persons in the city the ancient marks of distinction used by their families; as the collar from Torquatus [441]; from Cincinnatus the curl of (276) hair [442]; and from Cneius Pompey, the surname of Great, belonging to that ancient family. Ptolemy, mentioned before, whom he invited from his kingdom, and received with great honours, he suddenly put to death, for no other reason, but because he observed that upon entering the theatre, at a public exhibition, he attracted the eyes of all the spectators, by the splendour of his purple robe. As often as he met with handsome men, who had fine heads of hair, he would order the back of their heads to be shaved, to make them appear ridiculous. There was one Esius Proculus, the son of a centurion of the first rank, who, for his great stature and fine proportions, was called the Colossal. Him he ordered to be dragged from his seat in the arena, and matched with a gladiator in light armour, and afterwards with another completely armed; and upon his worsting them both, commanded him forthwith to be bound, to be led clothed in rags up and down the streets of the city, and, after being exhibited in that plight to the women, to be then butchered. There was no man of so abject or mean condition, whose excellency in any kind he did not envy. The Rex Nemorensis [443] having many years enjoyed the honour of the priesthood, he procured a still stronger antagonist to oppose him. One Porius, who fought in a chariot [444], having been victorious in an exhibition, and in his joy given freedom to a slave, was applauded so vehemently, that Caligula rose in such haste from his seat, that, treading upon the hem of his toga, he tumbled down the steps, full of indignation, (277) and crying out, "A people who are masters of the world, pay greater respect to a gladiator for a trifle, than to princes admitted amongst the gods, or to my own majesty here present amongst them."

XXXVI. He never had the least regard either to the chastity of his own person, or that of others. He is said to have been inflamed with an unnatural passion for Marcus Lepidus Mnester, an actor in pantomimes, and for certain hostages; and to have engaged with them in the practice of mutual pollution. Valerius Catullus, a young man of a consular family, bawled aloud in public that he had been exhausted by him in that abominable act. Besides his incest with his sisters, and his notorious passion for Pyrallis, the prostitute, there was hardly any lady of distinction with whom he did not make free. He used commonly to invite them with their husbands to supper, and as they passed by the couch on which he reclined at table, examine them very closely, like those who traffic in slaves; and if any one from modesty held down her face, he raised it up with his hand. Afterwards, as often as he was in the humour, he would quit the room, send for her he liked best, and in a short time return with marks of recent disorder about them. He would then commend or disparage her in the presence of the company, recounting the charms or defects of her person and behaviour in private. To some he sent a divorce in the name of their absent husbands, and ordered it to be registered in the public acts.

XXXVII. In the devices of his profuse expenditure, he surpassed all the prodigals that ever lived; inventing a new kind of bath, with strange dishes and suppers, washing in precious unguents, both warm and cold, drinking pearls of immense value dissolved in vinegar, and serving up for his guests loaves and other victuals modelled in gold; often saying, "that a man ought either to be a good economist or an emperor." Besides, he scattered money to a prodigious amount among the people, from the top of the Julian Basilica [445], during several days successively. He built two ships with ten banks of oars, after the Liburnian fashion, the poops of which blazed with jewels, and the sails were of various parti-colours. They were fitted up with ample baths, galleries, and saloons, and supplied with a great variety of vines and other fruit-trees. In these he would sail in the day-time along the coast of Campania, feasting (278) amidst dancing and concerts of music. In building his palaces and villas, there was nothing he desired to effect so much, in defiance of all reason, as what was considered impossible. Accordingly, moles were formed in the deep and adverse sea [446], rocks of the hardest stone cut away, plains raised to the height of mountains with a vast mass of earth, and the tops of mountains levelled by digging; and all these were to be executed with incredible speed, for the least remissness was a capital offence. Not to mention particulars, he spent enormous sums, and the whole treasures which had been amassed by Tiberius Caesar, amounting to two thousand seven hundred millions of sesterces, within less than a year.

XXXVIII. Having therefore quite exhausted these funds, and being in want of money, he had recourse to plundering the people, by every mode of false accusation, confiscation, and taxation, that could be invented. He declared that no one had any right to the freedom of Rome, although their ancestors had acquired it for themselves and their posterity, unless they were sons; for that none beyond that degree ought to be considered as posterity. When the grants of the Divine Julius and Augustus were produced to him, he only said, that he was very sorry they were obsolete and out of date. He also charged all those with making false returns, who, after the taking of the census, had by any means whatever increased their property. He annulled the wills of all who had been centurions of the first rank, as testimonies of their base ingratitude, if from the beginning of Tiberius's reign they had not left either that prince or himself their heir. He also set aside the wills of all others, if any person only pretended to say, that they designed at their death to leave Caesar their heir. The public becoming terrified at this proceeding, he was now appointed joint-heir with their friends, and in the case of parents with their children, by persons unknown to him. Those who lived any considerable time after making such a will, he said, were only making game of him; and accordingly he sent many of them poisoned cakes. He used to try such causes himself; fixing previously the sum he proposed to raise during the sitting, and, after he had secured it, quitting the tribunal. Impatient of the least delay, he condemned by a single sentence forty (279) persons, against whom there were different charges; boasting to Caesonia when she awoke, "how much business he had dispatched while she was taking her mid-day sleep." He exposed to sale by auction, the remains of the apparatus used in the public spectacles; and exacted such biddings, and raised the prices so high, that some of the purchasers were ruined, and bled themselves to death. There is a well-known story told of Aponius Saturninus, who happening to fall asleep as he sat on a bench at the sale, Caius called out to the auctioneer, not to overlook the praetorian personage who nodded to him so often; and accordingly the salesman went on, pretending to take the nods for tokens of assent, until thirteen gladiators were knocked down to him at the sum of nine millions of sesterces [447], he being in total ignorance of what was doing.

XXXIX. Having also sold in Gaul all the clothes, furniture, slaves, and even freedmen belonging to his sisters, at prodigious prices, after their condemnation, he was so much delighted with his gains, that he sent to Rome for all the furniture of the old palace [448]; pressing for its conveyance all the carriages let to hire in the city, with the horses and mules belonging to the bakers, so that they often wanted bread at Rome; and many who had suits at law in progress, lost their causes, because they could not make their appearance in due time according to their recognizances. In the sale of this furniture, every artifice of fraud and imposition was employed. Sometimes he would rail at the bidders for being niggardly, and ask them "if they were not ashamed to be richer than he was?" at another, he would affect to be sorry that the property of princes should be passing into the hands of private persons. He had found out that a rich provincial had given two hundred thousand sesterces to his chamberlains for an underhand invitation to his table, and he was much pleased to find that honour valued at so high a rate. The day following, as the same person was sitting at the sale, he sent him some bauble, for which he told him he must pay two hundred thousand sesterces, and "that he should sup with

Caesar upon his own invitation."

(280) XL. He levied new taxes, and such as were never before known, at first by the publicans, but afterwards, because their profit was enormous, by centurions and tribunes of the pretorian guards; no description of property or persons being exempted from some kind of tax or other. For all eatables brought into the city, a certain excise was exacted: for all law-suits or trials in whatever court, the fortieth part of the sum in dispute; and such as were convicted of compromising litigations, were made liable to a penalty. Out of the daily wages of the porters, he received an eighth, and from the gains of common prostitutes, what they received for one favour granted. There was a clause in the law, that all bawds who kept women for prostitution or sale, should be liable to pay, and that marriage itself should not be exempted.

XLI. These taxes being imposed, but the act by which they were levied never submitted to public inspection, great grievances were experienced from the want of sufficient knowledge of the law. At length, on the urgent demands of the Roman people, he published the law, but it was written in a very small hand, and posted up in a corner, so that no one could make a copy of it. To leave no sort of gain untried, he opened brothels in the Palatium, with a number of cells, furnished suitably to the dignity of the place; in which married women and free-born youths were ready for the reception of visitors. He sent likewise his nomenclators about the forums and courts, to invite people of all ages, the old as well as the young, to his brothel, to come and satisfy their lusts; and he was ready to lend his customers money upon interest; clerks attending to take down their names in public, as persons who contributed to the emperor's revenue. Another method of raising money, which he thought not below his notice, was gaming; which, by the help of lying and perjury, he turned to considerable account. Leaving once the management of his play to his partner in the game, he stepped into the court, and observing two rich Roman knights passing by, he ordered them immediately to be seized, and their estates confiscated. Then returning, in great glee, he boasted that he had never made a better throw in his life.

XLII. After the birth of his daughter, complaining of his (281) poverty, and the burdens to which he was subjected, not only as an emperor, but a father, he made a general collection for her maintenance and fortune. He likewise gave public notice, that he would receive new-year's gifts on the calends of January following; and accordingly stood in the vestibule of his house, to clutch the presents which people of all ranks threw down before him by handfuls and lapfuls. At last, being seized with an invincible desire of feeling money, taking off his slippers, he repeatedly walked over great heaps of gold coin spread upon the spacious floor, and then laying himself down, rolled his whole body in gold over and over again.

XLIII. Only once in his life did he take an active part in military affairs, and then not from any set purpose, but during his journey to Mevania, to see the grove and river of Clitumnus [449]. Being recommended to recruit a body of Batavians, who attended him, he resolved upon an expedition into Germany. Immediately he drew together several legions, and auxiliary forces from all quarters, and made every where new levies with the utmost rigour. Collecting supplies of all kinds, such as never had been assembled upon the like occasion, he set forward on his march, and pursued it sometimes with so much haste and precipitation, that the pretorian cohorts were obliged, contrary to custom, to pack their standards on horses or mules, and so follow him. At other times, he would march so slow and luxuriously, that he was carried in a litter by eight men; ordering the roads to be swept by the people of the neighbouring towns, and sprinkled with water to lay the dust.

XLIV. On arriving at the camp, in order to show himself an active general, and severe disciplinarian, he cashiered the lieutenants who came up late with the auxiliary forces from different quarters. In reviewing the army, he deprived of their companies most of the centurions of the first rank, who had now served their legal time in the wars, and some whose time would have expired in a few days; alleging against them their age and infirmity; and railing at the covetous disposition (282) of the rest of them, he reduced the bounty due to those who had served out their time to the sum of six thousand sesterces. Though he only received the submission of Adminius, the son of Cunobeline, a British king, who being driven from his native country by his father, came over to him with a small body of troops [450], yet, as if the whole island had been surrendered to him, he dispatched magnificent letters to Rome, ordering the bearers to proceed in their carriages directly up to the forum and the senate-house, and not to deliver the letters but to the consuls in the temple of Mars, and in the presence of a full assembly of the senators.

XLV. Soon after this, there being no hostilities, he ordered a few Germans of his guard to be carried over and placed in concealment on the other side of the Rhine, and word to be brought him after dinner, that an enemy was advancing with great impetuosity. This being accordingly done, he immediately threw himself, with his friends, and a party of the pretorian knights, into the adjoining wood, where lopping branches from the trees, and forming trophies of them, he returned by torch-light, upbraiding those who did not follow him, with timorousness and cowardice; but he presented the companions, and sharers of his victory with crowns of a new form, and under a new name, having the sun, moon, and stars represented on them, and which he called Exploratoriae. Again, some hostages were by his order taken from the school, and privately sent off; upon notice of which he immediately rose from table, pursued them with the cavalry, as if they had run away, and coming up with them, brought them back in fetters; proceeding to an extravagant pitch of ostentation likewise in this military comedy. Upon his again sitting down to table, it being reported to him that the troops were all reassembled, he ordered them to sit down as they were, in their armour, animating them in the words of that well-known verse of Virgil:

(283) Durate, et vosmet rebus servate secundis.--Aen. 1. Bear up, and save yourselves for better days.

In the mean time, he reprimanded the senate and people of Rome in a very severe proclamation, "For revelling and frequenting the diversions of the circus and theatre, and enjoying themselves at their villas, whilst their emperor was fighting, and exposing himself to the greatest dangers."

XLVI. At last, as if resolved to make war in earnest, he drew up his army upon the shore of the ocean, with his balistae and other engines of war, and while no one could imagine what he intended to do, on a sudden commanded them to gather up the sea shells, and fill their helmets, and the folds of their dress with them, calling them "the spoils of the ocean due to the Capitol and the Palatium." As a monument of his success, he raised a lofty tower, upon which, as at Pharos [451], he ordered lights to be burnt in the night-time, for the direction of ships at sea; and then promising the soldiers a donative of a hundred denarii [452] a man, as if he had surpassed the most eminent examples of generosity, "Go your ways," said he, "and be merry: go, ye are rich."

XLVII. In making preparations for his triumph, besides the prisoners and deserters from the barbarian armies, he picked out the men of greatest stature in all Gaul, such as he said were fittest to grace a triumph, with some of the chiefs, and reserved them to appear in the procession; obliging them not only to dye their hair yellow, and let it grow long, but to learn the German language, and assume the names commonly used in that country. He ordered likewise the gallies in which he had entered the ocean, to be conveyed to Rome a great part of the way by land, and wrote to his comptrollers in the city, "to make proper preparations for a triumph against (284) his arrival, at as small expense as possible; but on a scale such as had never been seen before, since they had full power over the property of every one."

XLVIII. Before he left the province, he formed a design of the most horrid cruelty--to massacre the legions which had mutinied upon the death of Augustus, for seizing and detaining by force his father, Germanicus, their commander, and himself, then an infant, in the camp. Though he was with great difficulty dissuaded from this rash attempt, yet neither the most urgent entreaties nor representations could prevent him from persisting in the design of decimating these legions. Accordingly, he ordered them to assemble unarmed, without so much as their swords; and then surrounded them with armed horse. But finding that many of them, suspecting that violence was intended, were making off, to arm in their own defence, he quitted the assembly as fast as he could, and immediately marched for Rome; bending now all his fury against the senate, whom he publicly threatened, to divert the general attention from the clamour excited by his disgraceful conduct. Amongst other pretexts of offence, he complained that he was defrauded of a triumph, which was justly his due, though he had just before forbidden, upon pain of death, any honour to be decreed him.

XLIX. In his march he was waited upon by deputies from the senatorian order, entreating him to hasten his return. He replied to them, "I will come, I will come, and this with me," striking at the same time the hilt of his sword. He issued likewise this proclamation: "I am coming, but for those only who wish for me, the equestrian order and the people; for I shall no longer treat the senate as their fellow-citizen or prince." He forbad any of the senators to come to meet him; and either abandoning or deferring his triumph, he entered the city in ovation on his birth- day. Within four months from this period he was slain, after he had perpetrated enormous crimes, and while he was meditating the execution, if possible, of still greater. He had entertained a design of removing to Antium, and afterwards to Alexandria; having first cut off the flower of the equestrian and senatorian orders. This is placed beyond all question, by two books which were found in his cabinet (285) under different titles; one being called the sword, and the other, the dagger. They both contained private marks, and the names of those who were devoted to death. There was also found a large chest, filled with a variety of poisons which being afterwards thrown into the sea by order of Claudius, are said to have so infected the waters, that the fish were poisoned, and cast dead by the tide upon the neighbouring shores.

L. He was tall, of a pale complexion, ill-shaped, his neck and legs very slender, his eyes and temples hollow, his brows broad and knit, his hair thin, and the crown of the head bald. The other parts of his body were much covered with hair. On this account, it was reckoned a capital crime for any person to look down from above, as he was passing by, or so much as to name a goat. His countenance, which was naturally hideous and frightful, he purposely rendered more so, forming it before a mirror into the most horrible contortions. He was crazy both in body and mind, being subject, when a boy, to the falling sickness. When he arrived at the age of manhood, he endured fatigue tolerably well; but still, occasionally, he was liable to a faintness, during which he remained incapable of any effort. He was not insensible of the disorder of his mind, and sometimes had thoughts of retiring to clear his brain [453]. It is believed that his wife Caesonia administered to him a love potion which threw him into a frenzy. What most of all disordered him, was want of sleep, for he seldom had more than three or four hours' rest in a night; and even then his sleep was not sound, but disturbed by strange dreams; fancying, among other things, that a form representing the ocean spoke to him. Being therefore often weary with lying awake so long, sometimes he sat up in his bed, at others, walked in the longest porticos about the house, and from time to time, invoked and looked out for the approach of day.

LI. To this crazy constitution of his mind may, I think, very justly be ascribed two faults which he had, of a nature directly repugnant one to the other, namely, an excessive confidence and the most abject timidity. For he, who affected so (286) much to despise the gods, was ready to shut his eyes, and wrap up his head in his cloak at the slightest storm of thunder and lightning; and if it was violent, he got up and hid himself under his bed. In his visit to Sicily, after ridiculing many strange objects which that country affords, he ran away suddenly in the night from Messini, terrified by the smoke and rumbling at the summit of Mount Aetna. And though in words he was very valiant against the barbarians, yet upon passing a narrow defile in Germany in his light car, surrounded by a strong body of his troops, some one happening to say, "There would be no small consternation amongst us, if an enemy were to appear," he immediately mounted his horse, and rode towards the bridges in great haste; but finding them blocked up with camp-followers and baggage-waggons, he was in such a hurry, that he caused himself to be carried in men's hands over the heads of the crowd. Soon afterwards, upon hearing that the Germans were again in rebellion, he prepared to quit Rome, and equipped a fleet; comforting himself with this consideration, that if the enemy should prove victorious, and possess themselves of the heights of the Alps, as the Cimbri [454] had done, or of the city, as the Senones [455] formerly did, he should still have in reserve the transmarine provinces [456]. Hence it was, I suppose, that it occurred to his assassins, to invent the story intended to pacify the troops who mutinied at his death, that he had laid violent hands upon himself, in a fit of terror occasioned by the news brought him of the defeat of his army.

LII. In the fashion of his clothes, shoes, and all the rest of his dress, he did not wear what was either national, or properly civic, or peculiar to the male sex, or appropriate to mere mortals. He often appeared abroad in a short coat of stout cloth, richly embroidered and blazing with jewels, in a tunic with sleeves, and with bracelets upon his arms; sometimes all in silks and (287) habited like a woman; at other times in the crepidae or buskins; sometimes in the sort of shoes used by the light-armed soldiers, or in the sock used by women, and commonly with a golden beard fixed to his chin, holding in his hand a thunderbolt, a trident, or a caduceus, marks of distinction belonging to the gods only. Sometimes, too, he appeared in the habit of Venus. He wore very commonly the triumphal ornaments, even before his expedition, and sometimes the breast-plate of Alexander the Great, taken out of his coffin. [457]

LIII. With regard to the liberal sciences, he was little conversant in philology, but applied himself with assiduity to the study of eloquence, being indeed in point of enunciation tolerably elegant and ready; and in his perorations, when he was moved to anger, there was an abundant flow of words and periods. In speaking, his action was vehement, and his voice so strong, that he was heard at a great distance. When winding up an harangue, he threatened to draw "the sword of his lucubration," holding a loose and smooth style in such contempt, that he said Seneca, who was then much admired, "wrote only detached essays," and that "his language was nothing but sand without lime." He often wrote answers to the speeches of successful orators; and employed himself in composing accusations or vindications of eminent persons, who were impeached before the senate; and gave his vote for or against the party accused, according to his success in speaking, inviting the equestrian order, by proclamation, to hear him.

LIV. He also zealously applied himself to the practice of several other arts of different kinds, such as fencing, charioteering, singing, and dancing. In the first of these, he practised with the weapons used in war; and drove the chariot in circuses built in several places. He was so extremely fond of singing and dancing, that he could not refrain in the theatre from singing with the tragedians, and imitating the gestures of the actors, either by way of applause or correction. A night exhibition which he had ordered the day he was slain, was thought to be intended for no other reason, than to take the opportunity afforded by the licentiousness of the season, to make his first appearance upon the stage. Sometimes, also, (288) he danced in the night. Summoning once to the Palatium, in the second watch of the night [458], three men of consular rank, who feared the words from the message, he placed them on the proscenium of the stage, and then suddenly came bursting out, with a loud noise of flutes and castanets [459], dressed in a mantle and tunic reaching down to his heels. Having danced out a song, he retired. Yet he who had acquired such dexterity in other exercises, never learnt to swim.

LV. Those for whom he once conceived a regard, he favoured even to madness. He used to kiss Mnester, the pantomimic actor, publicly in the theatre; and if any person made the least noise while he was dancing, he would order him to be dragged from his seat, and scourged him with his own hand. A Roman knight once making some bustle, he sent him, by a centurion, an order to depart forthwith for Ostia [460], and carry a letter from him to king Ptolemy in Mauritania. The letter was comprised in these words: "Do neither good nor harm to the bearer." He made some gladiators captains of his German guards. He deprived the gladiators called Mirmillones of some of their arms. One Columbus coming off with victory in a combat, but being slightly wounded, he ordered some poison to be infused in the wound, which he thence called Columbinum. For thus it was certainly named with his own hand in a list of other poisons. He was so extravagantly fond of the party of charioteers whose colours were green [461], that he supped and lodged for some time constantly in the stable where their horses were kept. At a certain revel, he made a present of two millions of sesterces to one Cythicus, a driver of a chariot. The day before the Circensian games, he used to send his soldiers to enjoin silence in the (289) neighbourhood, that the repose of his horse Incitatus [462] might not be disturbed. For this favourite animal, besides a marble stable, an ivory manger, purple housings, and a jewelled frontlet, he appointed a house, with a retinue of slaves, and fine furniture, for the reception of such as were invited in the horse's name to sup with him. It is even said that he intended to make him consul.

LVI. In this frantic and savage career, numbers had formed designs for cutting him off; but one or two conspiracies being discovered, and others postponed for want of opportunity, at last two men concerted a plan together, and accomplished their purpose; not without the privity of some of the greatest favourites amongst his freedmen, and the prefects of the pretorian guards; because, having been named, though falsely, as concerned in one conspiracy against him, they perceived that they were suspected and become objects of his hatred. For he had immediately endeavoured to render them obnoxious to the soldiery, drawing his sword, and declaring, "That he would kill himself if they thought him worthy of death;" and ever after he was continually accusing them to one another, and setting them all mutually at variance. The conspirators having resolved to fall upon him as he returned at noon from the Palatine games, Cassius Chaerea, tribune of the pretorian guards, claimed the part of making the onset. This Chaerea was now an elderly man, and had been often reproached by Caius for effeminacy. When he came for the watchword, the latter would give "Priapus," or "Venus;" and if on any occasion he returned thanks, would offer him his hand to kiss, making with his fingers an obscene gesture.

LVII. His approaching fate was indicated by many prodigies. The statue of Jupiter at Olympia, which he had ordered to be taken down and brought to Rome, suddenly burst out into such a violent fit of laughter, that, the machines employed in the work giving way, the workmen took to their heels. When this accident happened, there came up a man named Cassius, who said that he was commanded in a dream to sacrifice a bull to Jupiter. The Capitol at Capua was (290) struck with lightning upon the ides of March [15th March] as was also, at Rome, the apartment of the chief porter of the Palatium. Some construed the latter into a presage that the master of the place was in danger from his own guards; and the other they regarded as a sign, that an illustrious person would be cut off, as had happened before on that day. Sylla, the astrologer, being, consulted by him respecting his nativity, assured him, "That death would unavoidably and speedily befall him." The oracle of Fortune at Antium likewise forewarned him of Cassius; on which account he had given orders for putting to death Cassius Longinus, at that time proconsul of Asia, not considering that Chaerea bore also that name. The day preceding his death he dreamt that he was standing in heaven near the throne of Jupiter, who giving him a push with the great toe of his right foot, he fell headlong upon the earth. Some things which happened the very day of his death, and only a little before it, were likewise considered as ominous presages of that event. Whilst he was at sacrifice, he was bespattered with the blood of a flamingo. And Mnester, the pantomimic actor, performed in a play, which the tragedian Neoptolemus had formerly acted at the games in which Philip, the king of Macedon, was slain. And in the piece called Laureolus, in which the principal actor, running out in a hurry, and falling, vomited blood, several of the inferior actors vying with each other to give the best specimen of their art, made the whole stage flow with blood. A spectacle had been purposed to be performed that night, in which the fables of the infernal regions were to be represented by Egyptians and Ethiopians.

LVIII. On the ninth of the calends of February [24th January], and about the seventh hour of the day, after hesitating whether he should rise to dinner, as his stomach was disordered by what he had eaten the day before, at last, by the advice of his friends, he came forth. In the vaulted passage through which he had to pass, were some boys of noble extraction, who had been brought from Asia to act upon the stage, waiting for him in a private corridor, and he stopped to see and speak to them; and had not the leader of the party said that he was suffering from cold, he would have gone back, and made them act immediately. Respecting what followed, (291) two different accounts are given. Some say, that, whilst he was speaking to the boys, Chaerea came behind him, and gave him a heavy blow on the neck with his sword, first crying out, "Take this:" that then a tribune, by name Cornelius Sabinus, another of the conspirators, ran him through the breast. Others say, that the crowd being kept at a distance by some centurions who were in the plot, Sabinus came, according to custom, for the word, and that Caius gave him "Jupiter," upon which Chaerea cried out, "Be it so!" and then, on his looking round, clove one of his jaws with a blow. As he lay on the ground, crying out that he was still alive [463], the rest dispatched him with thirty wounds. For the word agreed upon among them all was, "Strike again." Some likewise ran their swords through his privy parts. Upon the first bustle, the litter bearers came running in with their poles to his assistance, and, immediately afterwards, his German body guards, who killed some of the assassins, and also some senators who had no concern in the affair.

LIX. He lived twenty-nine years, and reigned three years, ten months, and eight days. His body was carried privately into the Lamian Gardens [464], where it was half burnt upon a pile hastily raised, and then had some earth carelessly thrown over it. It was afterwards disinterred by his sisters, on their return from banishment, burnt to ashes, and buried. Before this was done, it is well known that the keepers of the gardens were greatly disturbed by apparitions; and that not a night passed without some terrible alarm or other in the house where he was slain, until it was destroyed by fire. His wife Caesonia was killed with him, being stabbed by a centurion; and his daughter had her brains knocked out against a wall.

LX. Of the miserable condition of those times, any person (292) may easily form an estimate from the following circumstances. When his death was made public, it was not immediately credited. People entertained a suspicion that a report of his being killed had been contrived and spread by himself, with the view of discovering how they stood affected towards him. Nor had the conspirators fixed upon any one to succeed him. The senators were so unanimous in their resolution to assert the liberty of their country, that the consuls assembled them at first not in the usual place of meeting, because it was named after Julius Caesar, but in the Capitol. Some proposed to abolish the memory of the Caesars, and level their temples with the ground. It was particularly remarked on this occasion, that all the Caesars, who had the praenomen of Caius, died by the sword, from the Caius Caesar who was slain in the times of Cinna.

* * * * * *

Unfortunately, a great chasm in the Annals of Tacitus, at this period, precludes all information from that historian respecting the reign of Caligula; but from what he mentions towards the close of the preceding chapter, it is evident that Caligula was forward to seize the reins of government, upon the death of Tiberius, whom, though he rivalled him in his vices, he was far from imitating in his dissimulation. Amongst the people, the remembrance of Germanicus' virtues cherished for his family an attachment which was probably, increased by its misfortunes; and they were anxious to see revived in the son the popularity of the father. Considering, however, that Caligula's vicious disposition was already known, and that it had even been an inducement with Tiberius to procure his succession, in order that it might prove a foil to his own memory; it is surprising that no effort was made at this juncture to shake off the despotism which had been so intolerable in the last reign, and restore the ancient liberty of the republic. Since the commencement of the imperial dominion, there never had been any period so favourable for a counter-revolution as the present crisis. There existed now no Livia, to influence the minds of the senate and people in respect of the government; nor was there any other person allied to the family of Germanicus, whose countenance or intrigues could promote the views of Caligula. He himself was now only in the twenty-fifth year of his age, was totally inexperienced in the administration of public affairs, had never performed even the smallest service to his country, and was generally known to be of a character which (293) disgraced his illustrious descent. Yet, in spite of all these circumstances, such was the destiny of Rome, that his accession afforded joy to the soldiers, who had known him in his childhood, and to the populace in the capital, as well as the people in the provinces, who were flattered with the delusive expectation of receiving a prince who should adorn the throne with the amiable virtues of Germanicus.

It is difficult to say, whether weakness of understanding, or corruption of morals, were more conspicuous in the character of Caligula. He seems to have discovered from his earliest years an innate depravity of mind, which was undoubtedly much increased by defect of education. He had lost both his parents at an early period of life; and from Tiberius' own character, as well as his views in training the person who should succeed him on the throne, there is reason to think, that if any attention whatever was paid to the education of Caligula, it was directed to vitiate all his faculties and passions, rather than to correct and improve them. If such was really the object, it was indeed prosecuted with success.

The commencement, however, of his reign was such as by no means prognosticated its subsequent transition. The sudden change of his conduct, the astonishing mixture of imbecility and presumption, of moral turpitude and frantic extravagance, which he afterwards evinced; such as rolling himself over heaps of gold, his treatment of his horse Incitatus, and his design of making him consul, seem to justify a suspicion that his brain had actually been affected, either by the potion, said to have been given him by his wife Caesonia, or otherwise. Philtres, or love-potions, as they were called, were frequent in those times; and the people believed that they operated upon the mind by a mysterious and sympathetic power. It is, however, beyond a doubt, that their effects were produced entirely by the action of their physical qualities upon the organs of the body. They were usually made of the satyrion, which, according to Pliny, was a provocative. They were generally given by women to their husbands at bed-time; and it was necessary towards their successful operation, that the parties should sleep together. This circumstance explains the whole mystery. The philtres were nothing more than medicines of a stimulating quality, which, after exciting violent, but temporary effects, enfeebled the constitution, and occasioned nervous disorders, by which the mental faculties, as well as the corporeal, might be injured. That this was really the case with Caligula, seems probable, not only from the falling sickness, to which he was subject, but from the habitual wakefulness of which he complained.

(294) The profusion of this emperor, during his short reign of three years and ten months, is unexampled in history. In the midst of profound peace, without any extraordinary charges either civil or military, he expended, in less than one year, besides the current revenue of the empire, the sum of 21,796,875 pounds sterling, which had been left by Tiberius at his death. To supply the extravagance of future years, new and exorbitant taxes were imposed upon the people, and those too on the necessaries of life. There existed now amongst the Romans every motive that could excite a general indignation against the government; yet such was still the dread of imperial power, though vested in the hands of so weak and despicable a sovereign, that no insurrection was attempted, nor any extensive conspiracy formed; but the obnoxious emperor fell at last a sacrifice to a few centurions of his own guard.

This reign was of too short duration to afford any new productions in literature; but, had it been extended to a much longer period, the effects would probably have been the same. Polite learning never could flourish under an emperor who entertained a design of destroying the writings of Virgil and Livy. It is fortunate that these, and other valuable productions of antiquity, were too widely diffused over the world, and too carefully preserved, to be in danger of perishing through the frenzy of this capricious barbarian.

FOOTNOTES:

[377] A.U.C. 757.

[378] A.U.C. 765.

[379] A.U.C. 770.

[380] A.U.C. 767.

[381] A.U.C. 771.

[382] This opinion, like some others which occur in Suetonius, may justly be considered as a vulgar error; and if the heart was found entire, it must have been owing to the weakness of the fire, rather than to any quality communicated to the organ, of resisting the power of that element.

[383] The magnificent title of King of Kings has been assumed, at different times, by various potentates. The person to whom it is here applied, is the king of Parthia. Under the kings of Persia, and even under the Syro-Macedonian kings, this country was of no consideration, and reckoned a part of Hyrcania. But upon the revolt of the East from the Syro-Macedonians, at the instigation of Arsaces, the Parthians are said to have conquered eighteen kingdoms.

[384] A.U.C. 765.

[385] It does not appear that Gaetulicus wrote any historical work, but Martial, Pliny, and others, describe him as a respectable poet.

[386] Supra Confluentes. The German tribe here mentioned occupied the country between the Rhine and the Meuse, and gave their name to Treves (Treviri), its chief town. Coblentz had its ancient name of Confluentes, from its standing at the junction of the two rivers. The exact site of the village in which Caligula was born is not known. Cluverius conjectures that it may be Capelle.

[387] Chap. vii.

[388] The name was derived from Caliga, a kind of boot, studded with nails, used by the common soldiers in the Roman army.

[389] According to Tacitus, who gives an interesting account of these occurrences, Treves was the place of refuge to which the young Caius was conveyed.--Annal. i.

[390] In c. liv. of TIBERIUS, we have seen that his brothers Drusus and Nero

fell a sacrifice to these artifices.

[391] Tiberius, who was the adopted father of Germanicus.

[392] Natriceus, a water-snake, so called from nato, to swim. The allusion is probably to Caligula's being reared in the island of Capri.

[393] As Phaeton is said to have set the world on fire.

[394] See the Life of TIBERIUS, c. lxxiii.

[395] His name also was Tiberius. See before, TIBERIUS, c. lxxvi.

[396] Procida, Ischia, Capri, etc.

[397] The eagle was the standard of the legion, each cohort of which had its own ensign, with different devices; and there were also little images of the emperors, to which divine honours were paid.

[398] See before, cc. liii. liv.

[399] See TIBERIUS, c. x.; and note.

[400] The mausoleum built by Augustus, mentioned before in his Life, c. C.

[401] The Carpentum was a carriage, commonly with two wheels, and an arched covering, but sometimes without a covering; used chiefly by matrons, and named, according to Ovid, from Carmenta, the mother of Evander. Women were prohibited the use of it in the second Punic war, by the Oppian law, which, however, was soon after repealed. This chariot was also used to convey the images of the illustrious women to whom divine honours were paid, in solemn processions after their death, as in the present instance. It is represented on some of the sestertii.

[402] See cc. xiv. and xxiii. of the present History.

[403] Ib. cc. vii. and xxiv.

[404] Life of TIBERIUS, c. xliii.

[405] See the Life of AUGUSTUS, cc. xxviii. and ci.

[406] Julius Caesar had shared it with them (c. xli.). Augustus had only kept up the form (c. xl.). Tiberius deprived the Roman people of the last remains of the freedom of suffrage.

[407] The city of Rome was founded on the twenty-first day of April, which was called Palilia, from Pales, the goddess of shepherds, and ever afterwards kept as a festival.

[408] A.U.C. 790.

[409] A.U.C. 791.

[410] A.U.C. 793.

[411] A.U.C. 794.

[412] The Saturnalia, held in honour of Saturn, was, amongst the Romans, the most celebrated festival of the whole year, and held in the month of December. All orders of the people then devoted themselves to mirth and feasting; friends sent presents to one another; and masters treated their slaves upon a footing of equality. At first it was held only for one day, afterwards for three days, and was now prolonged by Caligula's orders.

[413] See AUGUSTUS, cc. xxix and xliii. The amphitheatre of Statilius Taurus is supposed to have stood in the Campus Martius, and the elevation now called the Monte Citorio, to have been formed by its ruins.

[414] Supposed to be a house, so called, adjoining the Circus, in which some of the emperor's attendants resided.

[415] Now Puzzuoli, on the shore of the bay of Naples. Every one knows what wealth was lavished here and at Baiae, on public works and the marine villas of the luxurious Romans, in the times of the emperors.

[416] The original terminus of the Appian Way was at Brundusium. This mole formed what we should call a nearer station to Rome, on the same road, the ruins of which are still to be seen. St. Paul landed there.

[417] Essedis: they were light cars, on two wheels, constructed to carry only one person; invented, it is supposed, by the Belgians, and by them introduced into Britain, where they were used in war. The Romans, after their expeditions in Gaul and Britain, adopted this useful vehicle instead of their more cumbrous RHEDA, not only for journeys where dispatch was required, but in solemn processions, and for ordinary purposes. They seem to have become the fashion, for Ovid tells us that these little carriages were driven by young ladies, themselves holding the reins, Amor. xi. 16. 49.

[418] Suetonius flourished about seventy years after this, in the reign of Adrian, and derived many of the anecdotes which give interest to his history from cotemporary persons. See CLAUDIUS, c. xv. etc.

[419] See TIBERIUS, c. xlvii. and AUGUSTUS, c. xxxi.

[420] This aqueduct, commenced by Caligula and completed by Claudian, a truly imperial work, conveyed the waters of two streams to Rome, following the valley of the Anio from above Tivoli. The course of one of these rivulets was forty miles, and it was carried on arches, immediately after quitting its source, for a distance of three miles. The other, the Anio Novus, also began on arches, which continued for upwards of twelve miles. After this, both were conveyed under ground; but at the distance of six miles from the city, they

were united, and carried upon arches all the rest of the way. This is the most perfect of all the ancient aqueducts; and it has been repaired, so as to convey the Acqua Felice, one of the three streams which now supply Rome. See CLAUDIUS, c. xx.

[421] By Septa, Suetonius here means the huts or barracks of the pretorian camp, which was a permanent and fortified station. It stood to the east of the Viminal and Quirinal hills, between the present Porta Pia and S. Lorenzo, where there is a quadrangular projection in the city walls marking the site. The remains of the Amphitheatrum Castrense stand between the Porta Maggiore and S. Giovanni, formerly without the ancient walls, but now included in the line. It is all of brick, even the Corinthian pillars, and seems to have been but a rude structure, suited to the purpose for which it was built, the amusement of the soldiers, and gymnastic exercises. For this purpose they were used to construct temporary amphitheatres near the stations in the distant provinces, which were not built of stone or brick, but hollow circular spots dug in the ground, round which the spectators sat on the declivity, on ranges of seats cut in the sod. Many vestiges of this kind have been traced in Britain.

[422] The Isthmus of Corinth; an enterprize which had formerly been attempted by Demetrius, and which was also projected by Julius Caesar, c. xliv., and Nero, c. xix.; but they all failed of accomplishing it.

[423] On the authority of Dio Cassius and the Salmatian manuscript, this verse from Homer is substituted for the common reading, which is,

Eis gaian Danaon perao se. Into the land of Greece I will transport thee.

[424] Alluding, in the case of Romulus, to the rape of the Sabines; and in that of Augustus to his having taken Livia from her husband.-- AUGUSTUS, c. lxii.

[425] Selene was the daughter of Mark Antony by Cleopatra.

[426] See c. xii.

[427] The vast area of the Roman amphitheatres had no roof, but the audience were protected against the sun and bad weather by temporary hangings stretched over it.

[428] A proverbial expression, meaning, without distinction.

[429] The islands off the coast of Italy, in the Tuscan sea and in the Archipelago, were the usual places of banishment. See before, c. xv.; and in TIBERIUS, c. liv., etc.

[430] Anticyra, an island in the Archipelago, was famous for the growth of hellebore. This plant being considered a remedy for insanity, the proverb arose--Naviga in Anticyram, as much as to say, "You are mad."

[431] Meaning the province in Asia, called Galatia, from the Gauls who conquered it, and occupied it jointly with the Greek colonists.

[432] A quotation from the tragedy of Atreus, by L. Attius, mentioned by Cicero. Off. i. 28.

[433] See before, AUGUSTUS, c. lxxi.

[434] These celebrated words are generally attributed to Nero; but Dio and Seneca agree with Suetonius in ascribing them to Caligula.

[435] Gladiators were distinguished by their armour and manner of fighting. Some were called Secutores, whose arms were a helmet, a shield, a sword, or a leaden ball. Others, the usual antagonists of the former, were named Retiarii. A combatant of this class was dressed in a short tunic, but wore nothing on his head. He carried in his left hand a three-pointed lance, called Tridens or Fuscina, and in his right, a net, with which he attempted to entangle his adversary, by casting it over his head, and suddenly drawing it together; when with his trident he usually slew him. But if he missed his aim, by throwing the

net either too short or too far, he instantly betook himself to flight, and endeavoured to prepare his net for a second cast. His antagonist, in the mean time, pursued, to prevent his design, by dispatching him.

[436] AUGUSTUS, c. xxiii.

[437] TIBERIUS, c. xl.

[438] See before, c. xix.

[439] Popae were persons who, at public sacrifices, led the victim to the altar. They had their clothes tucked up, and were naked to the waist. The victim was led with a slack rope, that it might not seem to he brought by force, which was reckoned a bad omen. For the same reason, it was allowed to stand loose before the altar, and it was thought a very unfavourable sign if it got away.

[440] Plato de Repub. xi.; and Cicero and Tull. xlviii.

[441] The collar of gold, taken from the gigantic Gaul who was killed in single combat by Titus Manlius, called afterwards Torquatus, was worn by the lineal male descendants of the Manlian family. But that illustrious race becoming extinct, the badge of honour, as well as the cognomen of Torquatus, was revived by Augustus, in the person of Caius Nonius Asprenas, who perhaps claimed descent by the female line from the family of Manlius.

[442] Cincinnatus signifies one who has curled or crisped hair, from which Livy informs us that Lucius Quintus derived his cognomen. But of what badge of distinction Caligula deprived the family of the Cincinnati, unless the natural feature was hereditary, and he had them all shaved--a practice we find mentioned just below--history does not inform us, nor are we able to conjecture.

[443] The priest of Diana Nemorensis obtained and held his office by his prowess in arms, having to slay his competitors, and offer human sacrifices,

and was called Rex from his reigning paramount in the adjacent forest. The temple of this goddess of the chase stood among the deep woods which clothe the declivities of the Alban Mount, at a short distance from Rome--nemus signifying a grove. Julius Caesar had a residence there. See his Life, c. lxxi. The venerable woods are still standing, and among them chestnut-trees, which, from their enormous girth and vast apparent age, we may suppose to have survived from the era of the Caesars. The melancholy and sequestered lake of Nemi, deep set in a hollow of the surrounding woods, with the village on its brink, still preserve the name of Nemi.

[444] An Essedarian was one who fought from an Esseda, the light carriage described in a former note, p. 264.

[445] See before, JULIUS, c. x., and note.

[446] Particularly at Baiae, see before, c. xix. The practice of encroaching on the sea on this coast, commenced before,--

Jactis in altum molibus.--Hor. Od. B. iii. 1. 34.

[447] Most of the gladiators were slaves.

[448] The part of the Palatium built or occupied by Augustus and Tiberius.

[449] Mevania, a town of Umbria. Its present name is Bevagna. The Clitumnus is a river in the same country, celebrated for the breed of white cattle, which feed in the neighbouring pastures.

[450] Caligula appears to have meditated an expedition to Britain at the time of his pompous ovation at Puteoli, mentioned in c. xiii.; but if Julius Caesar could gain no permanent footing in this island, it was very improbable that a prince of Caligula's character would ever seriously attempt it, and we shall presently see that the whole affair turned out a farce.

[451] It seems generally agreed, that the point of the coast which was signalized by the ridiculous bravado of Caligula, somewhat redeemed by the erection of a lighthouse, was Itium, afterwards called Gessoriacum, and Bononia (Boulogne), a town belonging to the Gaulish tribe of the Morini; where Julius Caesar embarked on his expedition, and which became the usual place of departure for the transit to Britain.

[452] The denarius was worth at this time about seven pence or eight pence of our money.

[453] Probably to Anticyra. See before, c. xxix. note

[454] The Cimbri were German tribes on the Elbe, who invaded Italy A.U.C. 640, and were defeated by Metellus.

[455] The Senones were a tribe of Cis-Alpine Gauls, settled in Umbria, who sacked and pillaged Rome A.U.C. 363.

[456] By the transmarine provinces, Asia, Egypt, etc., are meant; so that we find Caligula entertaining visions of an eastern empire, and removing the seat of government, which were long afterwards realized in the time of Constantine.

[457] See AUGUSTUS, c. xviii.

[458] About midnight, the watches being divided into four.

[459] Scabella: commentators are undecided as to the nature of this instrument. Some of them suppose it to have been either a sort of cymbal or castanet, but Pitiscus in his note gives a figure of an ancient statue preserved at Florence, in which a dancer is represented with cymbals in his hands, and a kind of wind instrument attached to the toe of his left foot, by which it is worked by pressure, something in the way of an accordion.

[460] The port of Rome.

[461] The Romans, in their passionate devotion to the amusements of the circus and the theatre, were divided into factions, who had their favourites among the racers and actors, the former being distinguished by the colour of the party to which they belonged. See before, c. xviii., and TIBERIUS, c. xxxvii.

[462] In the slang of the turf, the name of Caligula's celebrated horse might, perhaps, be translated "Go a-head."

[463] Josephus, who supplies us with minute details of the assassination of Caligula, says that he made no outcry, either disdaining it, or because an alarm would have been useless; but that he attempted to make his escape through a corridor which led to some baths behind the palace. Among the ruins on the Palatine hill, these baths still attract attention, some of the frescos being in good preservation. See the account in Josephus, xix. 1, 2.

[464] The Lamian was an ancient family, the founders of Formiae. They had gardens on the Esquiline mount.

###

Printed in Great Britain
by Amazon